How to create a personal brand without spending a fortune

Affordable and simple ways to promote yourself or business

Humphrey Snyder

Table of Contents

Introduction

Why build a personal brand?

We live in an era overflowing with content. With content being consumed at such a fast pace over the last decade that people who had content made fortunes. With content in such high demand, software and resources to create content fast and cheap flooded the market.

Apps, article spinners and outsourcing to third world countries and having people who barely speak English create content has buried quality content under a pile of rubbish. At the same time, society has begun to not only doubt all the content available but also the owners of that content.

As fake news and other labels have gone viral, it is no wonder that it is harder than ever to establish authority and trust.

What does this have to do with a personal brand versus a business or corporate brand?

People arc trained to trust authority figures aka people in authority. At the same time, we have learned to doubt the sincerity and trustworthiness of businesses and politicians.

This means that you can build trust and authority as a person faster, easier and for less money than you could build that same credibility for a business. At the same time, it is simpler to establish an individual's authority on a subject than it is a business.

What does this mean?

It means that in most instances you will be better off building a personal brand around yourself than you would trying to build a corporate or business brand.

What is the key difference between a personal brand and a business brand if you own and essentially are the business?

A business should always have a separate identity from the owner of the business. Take Sam Walton, the founder of Wal-Mart & Sam's Club. His brand identity was a fatherly caring family man. Someone who cared about his fellow people.

Since he passed, I have heard many times how he would not countenance many of the negative things the corporate brands of Wal-Mart and Sam's Clubs have been accused of or seen doing. This is the power of the personal brand!

How to use this book.

This book is broken into chapters that are designed to help you understand a personal brand identity, the many ways to create one and how to select the methods that will work best for your own personal brand. Then in summation we will go over ways to continue building your brand identity over time without spending large amounts of time on it.

Chapter 1:

Developing a personal brand first then using it to help establish a business brand.

Developing a personal brand is not done overnight. It takes dedication and a commitment to put yourself out there so others can get to know you. At the same time there is always the question of what to share and where to share it.

In this chapter, we will go over why creating a personal brand does not mean you will not need or want a business or professional brand as well. In addition, we will discuss why creating the personal brand first is so beneficial.

Profiles on social media or other websites have become useful for people who want to hire a specific person. Usually these sites act like a person or company's brand. If the brand is not very flattering to the individual or company, then that individual or company will lose business.

Make sure that the brand you represent is more like what you want for the brand than what you do not want it to be. It must make people think that they want to hire you because of your brand and how it represents you.

Creating the proper brand using the social media of today must be focused on you and your work, not someone else's. After all, it is part of business. There is nothing wrong with developing your brand.

Are You a Freelancer?

As a freelancer, your brand is everything! Your work is practically your life. By representing your brand, you're representing yourself. Everywhere you go, your brand is there to help you gain jobs and then some.

Building yourself up as an expert helps to reach clients who want to use your skills and buying your time because of that. If you undersell yourself, then you will have to resort to a third-party representative to sell your brand instead of relying on your own mind.

Make sure to have a website, logo, tagline or some other tool to boast your brand. Some of these are free to use to help you save money while creating your brand.

Run a Small Business?

If you own and run a small business, it can be easy to lose control of your company. If you have to hire another professional to help you run the business, then you do not know all of the problems that have arisen while in the field or the office thereby having no control over anything. To remedy this, making your business brand more visible to clients than your personal brand will help keep your business running without your undivided attention all day every day.

An Employee?

The problem for an employee of any business is you sometimes need to leave your job for a few hours to be yourself without having to worry if your representation of your company's brand is appropriate. With our world being overrun by smart phones and new technology being created every day, you could find yourself ruining your business chances with a misrepresented post.

Avoiding terrible situations where you do something inappropriate in public will keep your company's brand from being tainted. Depending on the business you work for, connecting your work and life can be beneficial.

When an employee makes a public mistake like writing a racist joke or telling one in front of a person of a different race, then they are misrepresenting their brand. This usually results in the person being fired from their job. This is a huge mistake and you could lose other job opportunities.

An Authentic Brand, Whether It is a Business One or Personal One

By remaining true to your brand, then everything will begin to fall into place and you will not need to look over your shoulder for problems. Keeping your social media accounts up to date will help you develop an authentic brand but keep an eye out for any mistakes you will undoubtedly make.

When dealing with creating a personal or business brand, it helps to remember that both are important for different reasons. It all depends on how you want to represent yourself as a business or as an individual. Just make sure not to forget to make your brand representable.

Building a personal brand is one of many useful things you can do to start selling your work and yourself. After all, a personal brand is powerful and valuable but takes quite a bit of work to get just right. Besides, one person's personal brand grows as they continue building it rather than as they continue to achieve success in their chosen niche.

Just like building a business from the ground up, you have to build your personal brand from scratch. You have to find clients who are looking for someone in a specific field of expertise, decide which marketing methods to use and continue delivering the work the clients ask for when they hire you. The rewards are worth every effort you have put in for the clients.

As your brand continues to grow, clients start to pop out of the woodwork and you are able to close more deals thereby growing more prospects than when you had started out. The statistics are outstanding. Business to business consumers only speak to a person selling their skills after the online research is completed only 77% of the time. However only slightly more than fifty percent narrow down the potential seller based on the online research. All it takes is a bit of careful planning before trying to promote your personal brand.

To get started selling your personal brand once it is built, here are a few things you could do to get potential clients.

One is headshots or profile pictures.

The era of Glamour shots as long since become a thing of the past. Using a professional portrait is rarely used in promoting your brand. However, as you begin to advocate your brand, using a head shot will give potential clients a face to put to a business. Just make sure they are up-to-date as your business or brand grows.

Let's say that you are promoting your dog training skills. Then you can take a picture of yourself with your own dog or have a friend take a picture of you training your dog in obedience. However, don't take a picture of you with a cat or some other non-dog creature. That just makes potential clients skip over your flyer or online business website and move on to someone else.

Using the pictures you have taken of yourself for your brand on social media, a blog, a website or a bio if you are a writer will help you to represent your brand or business.

The second thing you can use to gain clients is your focus.

As an entrepreneur, you want to be known as an expert in your chosen niche. To do that, you need to recognize the one thing that sets you apart from others who are doing the same thing you are. You need to let potential clients know what you are passionate about and what you are an expert of so that they hire you. Here are a few questions to ask yourself:

What is your business focus and the angle you are trying to show potential clients?

What do you do as a business?

What's the vision you have for your business?

Your focus and the subsequent vision help to provide the basis for the steps you need to take to promote your brand.

The third thing to help you gain clients is your specific pitch.

When people meet in an elevator, one of two things happen: One, the occupants of said elevator are quiet. Two, they strike up a conversation and one explains what they do for a living. A trip between two floors of a building while riding in an elevator usually takes about thirty seconds, which is not a lot of time to give a speech about your business.

Some people usually need more than thirty seconds to promote themselves. Business cards help to a certain extent but they are rarely as personal as actually telling someone all about your business or work. A short pitch is usually not just used to connect you to potential clients. You usually can create a short pitch on social media to explain what you do so that you gain some followers who just might know someone looking for what you do specifically.

To create your pitch, start by writing all the details of your brand or business. Once that is done, start shortening your details, making sure to keep a few of the important details in your pitch that still make potential clients want to use your skills for jobs.

For example, you do lawn service, mowing, trimming, pruning, etc. You want your pitch to tell potential clients why they should hire you instead of someone else. Just telling clients that you do yard work is not specific enough and just telling them about the things that do not advocate your lawn care services will make them not want to hire you. Giving enough details about your lawn care services while keeping it short will garner the clients you want to work for.

The fourth thing you can do to gain clients is by knowing your unique selling proposition (USP).

Your elevator pitch is not enough to sell your services. Your unique selling proposition (USP) helps with that. It sets you apart from people who are selling the same services you are. Your USP should tell potential clients why they should use your services and not someone else's. What makes you different from the rest? What is it that you do that is different from the rest? The USP is a single sentence that promotes you as a business owner, your main skill and how the client will benefit from you working for them.

There are three categories into which unique selling propositions fall: Quality, Price, and Service. Quality is about how superior your skills are whether it is special ingredients, unique craftsmanship or a specific trademark. Price is about how much money you are asking for your services that sets you apart from other sellers. Maybe you have lower prices for your services than others or you give discounts for repeat clients. Service is about how you conduct yourself. Maybe you have other services you can provide as an added bonus. Say a client asks you to mow their lawn but you notice that the bushes are way too overgrown. You tell your client that you will trim the bushes for free which makes them happy.

The fifth thing to help you gain clients is a well-defined audience.

When you target a specific clientele, then you are a few steps away from building the perfect brand. Your area of expertise and how it is defined is one part of your brand-building journey. If you have the right audience , then your brand is useful for gaining clients.

Without a target audience, you're basically throwing blindly. It is much like target practice. With arrows, the bull's eye of the target is more points. If you miss the bull's eye, then you are falling short of your target.

Once you know who you are targeting as an audience, then you are able to:

❖   Have content that is highly valuable to meet the specific needs of the clients

❖ Solve any problems that might arise with solutions that work

❖ Have advocates for your brand who will extol your services to others who will then buy your services

❖ Engage your audience with special offers for using your services and where to find them If you do not know your audience , then your brand will never grow bigger and more sought-after.

The sixth thing to help you gain clients is having the mindset of a student

Even when you have plenty of experience in your field, you still have more room for learning. Claiming that you are a student who needs to continue learning, will help you when change happens. Keeping up with trends as they happen is a great example of this. If you ignore the new trends, then you will lose clients. After all, learning new things, expanding your knowledge and developing new skills is good for building your brand. There are always opportunities to help your audience learn something new and more valuable.

The seventh thing you can do to gain clients is to have a spectacular marketing tactic.

Having a spectacular marketing strategy will help you promote yourself even before launching your brand. It helps to get your ducks in a row, so to speak. Your marketing strategy does not need to be as well-rounded as someone with a larger brand but it is still good to create one that fits you. Your marketing should include:

- Posting schedules on social media
- Plan for engaging your audience and influencing many clients
- An engagement strategy for your website and the websites of other people
- A marketing strategy for the content you provide, distribute and promote

The eighth thing you can do to gain clients is to have a review of your brand.

If you have information about you and your brand for potential clients to see, then you can review the services you provide and anything else that needs your attention. If there is anything that does not work well with your brand, then you can take action to remove the things that do not promote your brand. However, this review is not a one-time thing. You must continue to review your brand and make any changes that need addressed.

The ninth thing you need to do to gain more clients is to have a website that promotes your brand.

Your website not only caters to your brand but also to the clients you will gain. When people search for your name and brand, your website will be one of the top results they find. It ensures that you will always have clients. If you did not have a website, it makes it harder for clients to find you and you will quite possibly lose money than gain it.

The tenth thing you must do to gain clients is to define your own story.

Letting your clients know how you came to create your brand is one way to gain clients. Even those with big brands have done this. Clients who are interested in your brand will want to know more about you, both personal and professional. If you know how to do many things, then letting your clients know about your skills will be very useful. Your story will define you and your brand.

The eleventh thing you can do is to build on the feedback you have received.

The feedback you receive will help immensely when creating your brand. It provides the framework when you receive feedback from peers, family and the clients that you already have. You can also ask them a few questions about what they think you are good at, what weaknesses they think you have and what they think your strengths are.

Let's say that you have received negative feedback from someone you trust. Finding out what they found wrong with your services and fixing the problem is a good example of building your brand using feedback.

The twelfth thing you can do to gain clients is to clearly define your goals.

Why did you develop your brand? Does it create an image of you that will help you gain a better position in your jobs? Do you want a more professional look to help gain more clients?

By defining your goals from the get-go will help you shape your brand and your promotion and marketing direction. Besides defining your much larger goals, defining the smaller goals that you can easily attain is important as well. Breaking down your large goals into smaller objectives will help you achieve them faster.

The thirteenth thing you need to do to gain clients is to generate a personal style.

Most brands need a style guide to help them with their logos, colors and fonts for their brands to stand out while representing their services or products including their employee's dress code. By creating a style guide like the major brands, you can represent your brand better as you follow the guide you have made for yourself. This will include your look, the way you carry yourself as a business and how you interact with clients.

The fourteenth thing you must do to gain clients is to create a strategy for your content.

A content strategy is just as important as a regular marketing strategy because content is king when it comes to your brand. The content you use helps you to build your authority and shows that you are an expert in your field. Guest posts will help you to engender referrals and links to help with your content strategy as well as short videos sharing your business ideals.

You can maintain a steady schedule while creating just the right topics for engaging your audience while giving your brand a chance to grow and flourish.

The last fifteenth thing you need to do to gain clients through your brand is to evaluate the competition.

While building your brand is not about how popular it is, it is important to know where you stand in terms of competition. There are some data sites to help you determine where each of your competition is in terms of rank as well as where you are at on the list. In the beginning stages of your brand-building, there might not be any services you are wanting to provide for your clients. Knowing who your competition might be will be useful to know once you start selling your services.

Your competitors fall into two categories, direct and indirect competitors. Direct competitors are those who are going up against you for the money your audience will use to pay for your services while indirect competitors are those who are vying for your audience's attention.

It is a definite no-no to copy your competitors' methods. After all, you do not want to be part of the crowd but rather you want to stand out to your audience. You want to be ten times better than your competition because you are so much more than your brand.

Brand Awareness

If people do not know who you are exactly, how can they ever buy your digital products? Simple, they cannot.

Brand awareness is one of the most important aspects of developing an online business. Making sure people are aware of your brand and your products makes you even more likely to generate profit.

Learning to grow your brand will position your business for success, but you might not know where to start. That is where this chapter comes in.

This chapter is going to show you not only how to grow your brand on a budget, but also how to implement valuable, simple strategies to improve your brand awareness and get the word out about your products.

Of course, these strategies will not generate results overnight. But they will continue building momentum as you continue to create new online courses and continue to expand your brand to new enterprises.

6 Steps to Grow Your Brand on a Budget

When you are first starting out in Knowledge Commerce or branding, you likely do not have unlimited means or funds. You need to market your business if you are engrossed in growing your brand, but you have to pinch pennies in the process.

Your brand is not impossible to achieve. In fact, there are many ways to grow your brand while on a budget. There are six most cost-effective ways to increase your brand awareness without blowing your budget.

1. Get to Know Who Your Target Personas Are

Who do you want to serve with your business? What are the qualities they possess that make you want to tailor your brand to?

A buyer personage is a fictionalized biography of your perfect customer. It defines that person's goals, habits, problems, demographics, struggles, and other details so you can market to them more effectively than ever before.

Imagine how you would describe a character from your favorite TV show. Where does he/she work? What are the main causes of conflict in his/her life? How does he/she spend his/her time? How much money does he/she make? Where does he/she live?

Answering all of these questions will help you get to know who your ideal customer is more intimately. Consequently, each piece of content or copy you write will speak candidly to that person.

For instance, if your target customer is a young single mother with a full-time job and a little apartment or house, you would approach content differently than if you decided targeting a middle-aged family man with kids in college and a low-stress job. You must think like your customers if you want your products to appeal to them.

2. Develop Your Unique Brand Voice

A brand voice expresses how you sound to other people. It makes you more memorable and recognizable.

Have you ever visited and read Seth Godin's blog? It is an outstanding example of a consistent voice in Knowledge Commerce. His voice (sparse, inspiring, and question-oriented) translates really well into his books, his speeches, and other endeavors. He is amazing at metaphors, so he uses them liberally.

That is precisely the kind of consistency you want to build for your own Knowledge Commerce brand.

Your voice should resemble the way you would talk to a friend or family member. Are you naturally funny, tell lots of stories? Can you convey complex ideas in easy-to-understand ways?

In other words, go with your strengths by amplifying them in your writing and speaking so you come across as genuine and relatable.

3. Build a Consistent Social Media Presence While Online

Social media might be the new blog but blogging is not dead. However, there are benefits to social media.

Many of your customers and prospect customers hang out on social media. They catch up with friends, participate in memes and funny posts, and scroll for inspiration.

You want to be there for them when they arrive.

According to a study done by MarketingSherpa, about fifty-eight percent of respondents reported that they follow at least one brand on social media. Evidently, consumers do not just use social media to check in with people they know.

Begin by choosing the best social platforms for your Knowledge Commerce business. Do lots of your prospects hang out on Twitter, congregate on Facebook or are they sharing photos on Instagram?

Once you know which sites they use, then start building up your presence on those platforms. Follow prominent people in your industry, engage with people who discuss your chosen niche, and make your profile as professional as possible while still being yourself.

4. Start a Blog — And Keep It Updated

As mentioned before, blogging is not dead. Posts on blogs attract readers who might become customers in the future.

The point is that content marketing should serve as the foundation of your branding process. It is what demonstrates who you are and why you are in business for the world to see.

It is also a great way to show off your skills and knowledge.

Start a blog today if you have not done so already. More importantly, keep it updated constantly. Lots of entrepreneurs start blogs, then ignore them for weeks, months, or even years which is never good.

If someone were to come across your blog and discover you have not posted in six months, what might they think? They would assume that you are no longer in business, and then you would lose a customer.

Blogging has become essential for Knowledge Commerce professionals, so do not just start a blog, make sure to keep it updated. Share any news you might have about your business, share little-known tips with your audience or start a blog series to introduce a new online course.

5. Devote Yourself to Customer Service

Customer service really matters in every industry. When you do not offer great customer service, you begin to lose customers. It is that simple, really.

Your brand must revolve around on how you treat customers. Demonstrate that you're willing to answer questions, resolve complaints, and share your knowledge with the rest of the world.

Have you ever experienced a terrible customer service dilemma where you felt you had gotten the short end of the stick? Did you ever consider never patronizing that business again or boycotting it altogether?

That is not something you want from your customers. If they have a bad customer service experience from you, then they might just do the same thing. You want your customers to be satisfied with your services so that they keep coming back time and again.

6. Partner With Other Knowledge Commerce Professionals

Remember back in high school when you wanted to be part of the popular group? Maybe you were one of those students who were in the school band and wanted to be friends with the head cheerleader. What was it about the "it" crowd that made you want to be part of that?

The same goes for when building your brand. You see other more successful entrepreneurs doing better than you and you feel like you are in high school once again. You want to be part of their success. If your customers see you associating with bigger brands on social media, then they will want to be part of your successes.

It works like that in business, too. If people see that you're associated with another strong brand, your brand becomes stronger as a result.

That is why many companies post the logos or names of their customers on their websites. It is a form of social proof that they are part of the business "it" crowd. Don't you want to be part of it too?

Once you know how to boost your brand, then you can move onto more important things like having a brand-awareness strategy. By having a brand-awareness strategy in place, you can grow faster and manage your reputation more easily. Here are twenty-two brand-awareness strategies to fuel your imagination.

1. Host a Webinar

A live webinar or even one that is pre-recorded can be proven ways that are extremely beneficial to your brand. You are placed in front of a camera that allows you interact with your audience. Or you could just be in front of a microphone recorder and have a chat feature on your webinar where you can read the questions your listeners have and answer them while on-air.

Webinars are used to answer customers' questions, to exhibit a particular skill or process, provide tutorials, promote new digital products, or get them excited about your business. Don't be afraid to try new formats and to engage with your audience in real time.

By hosting a live webinar, you can make it available as a recording on your website or blog. It will continue to drive traffic and conversions long after the event has ended.

2. Start a Referral Program

A referral program encourages your customers to share your business with their friends and other associates. They could get a discount on your online courses, a free month of membership to your membership site, or some other advantage.

You get a new paying customer who might refer friends of their own as a result of this. While referral programs might seem costly, they actually multiply your revenue many times over.

Be sure to share details of your referral program on social media, your blog, and other online authorities.

3. Offer to Guest Blog

Content marketing not only works on owned media but on guest posting as well. Guest posting on other people's blogs can give you access to new audiences and generate backlinks for your personal brand website. Think of guest blogging as the Internet marketing's answer to visiting a physical business and handing out your business cards. It is more effective, though, because you have the chance to demonstrate your knowledge and your credibility.

4. Create and Share Infographics

Infographics are very shareable and engaging. You can use data and information you have collected on yourself or you have sourced from other websites.

Only the best infographics tell a story by helping the viewer better understand the subject or information so they can apply to their personal or professional lives.

Infographics that are data-driven are among the most popular. After all, would you rather not view dry data represented in graphic form than read a list of statistics?

5. Get Social With Your Customers

Social media is mostly used for interacting with others on a personal level, not just for linking to your latest blog posts or announcing the launch of the new online course. When your customers follow you on social media, interact with them through conversations, asking them questions, thanking them for their patronage, and answering their questions. When you share stories and otherwise socialize with your customers, they feel more embedded in your business. Subsequently, they will be more likely to buy your future digital products.

6. Surround Yourself With Influential People You Admire

Paying attention to how others do it is one of the best ways to grow your brand. After all, you are not trying to reinvent the wheel.

Additionally, if you surround yourself with people who are influential, consumers will begin to associate your name with theirs. As mentioned above, your brand can grow financially simply by association with a stronger brand. Wouldn't you want to make more money as a brand?

7. Take Advantage of LinkedIn Publishing

When you first start a website and a blog, you won't have many readers because nobody knows you exist yet. You can depend on unforced traffic to drive potential customers to your content, but that takes time. Speed up the process by circulating content on a platform that already has a built-in audience.

LinkedIn publishing is one key example. Everyone in your network will see your posts and can possibly share them with their own audiences. Not only that, people you do not know can find your content more easily and find ways to bond with you.

8. Start Your Own Medium Account or Publication

Another great way to find a broader audience is to publish on Medium, a blogging platform that allows anyone to have a voice.

Just sign up for your account on Medium, click your profile icon, and click "New Story." You can then write your article in the interface or paste an article that you have written elsewhere which makes it easy to grow an audience.

Medium has a large audience of highly involved consumers. You can easily build a following and drive customers to your website so they can check out your digital products because of this method.

9. Create a Podcast

Podcasts are a fantastic way to add more variety to your content-production strategy. Consumers can listen to them on the way to work, the gym, the grocery store or while they perform chores around the house.

A podcast should center around a specific theme. You can talk for ten minutes or no more than two hours, depending on your audience's preferences, and you can also host guests which lets your listeners hear someone besides you talk about your brand.

10. Try PPC Advertising

Pay-per-click (PPC) advertising is a faster way to build your brand and gain exposure. You get to set your budget, so you don't have to worry about breaking the bank, and you can hone your audience so your brand message only gets seen by people in your chosen demographics.

Keep in mind that PPC advertising works better for customers at the bottom of the funnel. Provide a "you cannot miss this" offer that will encourage consumers to click and, ultimately, buy your products.

11. Do not Neglect Content Marketing

Content marketing should be the epicenter of your brand-building activities. Without content, you have no way to bring in organic traffic which will drive down your business.

Keep in mind that content does not just have to be articles. You can optimize infographics, videos, quotes, and plenty of other content types for SEO (Search Engine Optimization) (which we will cover next).

Focus on putting out content on a regular basis. That way, your audience knows when to check back for new stuff and special offers.

12. Optimize Your Content for Search Engines

SEO or Search Engine Optimization is an essential skill for any online entrepreneur. Learn how to optimize your blog posts and other content for the search engines.

Use longer or specific keywords in your titles, body content and meta-descriptions. You can add them to subheadings, in addition, to boost your SEO.

Make sure to add alternate tags to your images so the search engines can understand them in context. Additionally, take the time to make sure the structure of your article is strong.

13. Try Remarketing Campaigns

Remarketing helps boost brand awareness by displaying your brand to people who have already encountered it before. It is like seeing a TV commercial, then seeing the same one (or one that is similar) the next day. You are more likely to remember the brand especially if that commercial plays over and over again throughout the day when you turn on the television.

14. Test Paid Social Advertising Strategies

Advertising on Instagram, Facebook, Twitter, and other social media sites can work just as well — if not better — than PPC (pay-per-click) advertising. It is also less costly in many scenarios.

Test social advertising using a small budget. See if you get a decent ROI or return on investment and if conversations about your business become more common. The goal is to urge people to become used to your brand image so they will remember what you do and how your business will benefit them.

15. Hold a Contest

A great way to get more people enthusiastic about your brand is to give something away for free. Maybe it is a free month of access to your membership site or perhaps it is free access to your latest mini-course. Either way, people love free stuff and giveaways.

Whatever the case may be, inspire people to spread the word about your contest, especially on social media.

You could offer double entries, for example, to people who retweet about the contest or multiple entries for posting the details of the contest on all social media platforms and signing up for a newsletter with more information. Just make sure that the giveaway relates directly to your business.

16. Tell The Story About How Your Brand Came To Be

People love to hear stories especially personal stories. Why else do they check in on their favorite television shows every week, buy books to read in their spare time, and relate personal anecdotes to their friends?

You can promote brand awareness by telling a compelling brand story. How did you acquire the knowledge you share? How did you come to know what you know? When and why did you start your business? What event in your life inspired you to share your information with the world?

It does not have to be an earth-shattering story. Your goal is to simply share a story that is emotionally driven to which readers can relate. Be sure to focus on experiences that your audience members might share.

17. Create Interactive Content For All

People love giving their opinions and interacting with websites. It generates what feels like a conversation even if the dialogue does not happen in real time.

Interactive content, like webinars, polls, quizzes, and surveys, are brilliant ways to drive user engagement. You can use them to give your audience a say in what product you will create next or what types of content you will distribute.

Just make sure that interactive content is easy to use. Many entrepreneurs benefit from creating fun interactive games, for instance, but only if the intended audience identify with how it works.

18. Enhance Your Email Signature

Every time you send an email, you are given an opportunity to grow your brand. Think about all the times you have seen an email signature on an inbound email and clicked on a link to see what it was all about.

Enhance your email signature for clicks. Do not just include a link to your website maybe add a call to action or CTA that induces people to check out what you offer.

19. Offer Early Access To Samples

Everyone likes being part of the inner circle. You could give your current customers a random sampling of your audience early access to one of your online courses.

For example, you could post on Facebook that the first thirty people to message you will receive early access. Alternatively, you could use a contest that directly involves sharing with other people to gain more entries for early access.

Whatever the case may be, your goal is to produce an exclusive bond with a smaller group of people. You will strengthen your brand as a result.

20. Establish a Members-Only Section of Your Website

Several years ago, the display ad model that was once used as a place for people to become members of something, broke down. Since then, membership sites have become progressively popular. Professionals of Knowledge Commerce cannot stay afloat just by running ads. They need a better way of generating income.

A membership site will provide exclusive content to people who pay the monthly or annual fee for access. You will send the message that you have valuable information to share, which will enhance and grow your brand image.

21. Start Your Own Language

Do you and your friends have inside jokes or made up words only you know the meaning of? Quite possibly! Even some of the strongest brands come from companies who have established their own language.

For instance, all the words people are using for other industries just did not reflect their potential and culture. Consequently, the moniker Knowledge Commerce was created. It suited those companies as well and has strengthened their brands.

You can do as well. This can be done within at least one day if not more.

22. Stop Trying to Please Everybody

Many entrepreneurs falsely believe a brand needs to have as many followers as possible. However, this is true for certain industries. For example, car manufacturers must need to have enormous followings to uphold their businesses.

It is different in Knowledge Commerce. You can benefit from a tiny pool of loyal customers who then buy each of your products and engage with your brand online. That is much better than having a huge social media following, for instance, that never produces any cash.

You cannot please everyone. Instead, focus on pleasing the people who share your values, interests, ideals, and beliefs. You will grow your brand with a group of intensely engaged customers who will want to know everything you know.

Conclusion:

The site, Kajabi offers you the tools you will need to build your brand around your digital products. All of these strategies work on the Kajabi platform, and you will not need many third-party tools to set your plan in motion.

They help their Kajabi Heroes build lasting brands around transparency, honesty, humor, knowledge sharing, and more. No matter the brand image you want created, you can do so with Kajabi.

Of course, your primary reason for existence revolves around your knowledge. You share what you know with others in exchange for money. That's the way Knowledge Commerce works.

For that reason, your personal brand and corporate brand are inextricably entwined. You will build your business based on your own knowledge and credibility in your field.

That is why it is completely essential to focus on brand awareness the minute you begin selling your digital products. If you do not shape and hone your brand image, you cannot control it.

Your brand lives whether you are aware of it or not. It is your job to make sure other people see you the way you want to be seen as a brand.

Understanding how to grow your brand will make your business a success faster and more proficiently. That is what we all want, right?

If you have not started boosting brand awareness for your business, now is the time to begin. Get to know who your ideal customers are. Develop and hone your brand voice. Get on social media, start your blog, and make sure you are offering all-star customer service.

You can also partner with other Knowledge Commerce professionals to strengthen your brand image through effective relationships.

Once you have those assets in place, try a few of these twenty-two strategies to build brand awareness.

Begin a referral program, guest blog on other sites, share some infographics, and surround yourself with influential people in your space. Consider publishing on other platforms, such as LinkedIn and Medium and Facebook as well.

You might want to create a podcast, host a webinar, and increase your social media activity. Paid advertising can also help with brand awareness. After all, you have to start somewhere.

In conclusion, the world will see your personal brand and buy your services based on that. Polishing the look of your brand is one way of doing this without ruining your money-making chances. Launching your brand with these elements guarantees that you will be able to connect with the right clients and brand audience. Once you reach your chosen people, they will pass on your wisdom to others who will then buy your services.

Chapter 2: YouTube

YouTube is the second most popular place to visit while on the Internet, right there sandwiched between *Google* and *Facebook*. Do you have a social media strategy for your personal branding? Then *YouTube* is a must-have to your strategy.

You still haven't considered personal branding? Well, let's start there. The concept of personal branding gained popularity after an article by Tom Peters. The article begins with an interesting headline: *The Brand Called You*. "Today, in the Age of the Individual, you have to be your own brand." That is how personal branding got started.

Personal branding is a marketing practice, which, promotes you and your skillsets as a brand. For example, you can build a brand around your name. All the pictures of beautiful fit people you find on Instagram, those are all part of a personal branding strategy, as well.

Now, the question is: why do you need a personal brand? Let us answer that question with an experiment: First, Google your name, and include your hometown in the keywords. This is so you'll get localized results. Would you like to improve the results people get when they search for your name? That is what personal branding is all about. It can benefit you in getting a better job. And will help you build an authoritative online persona.

Let's see how YouTube can help you with that. YouTube is the place where you can upload videos. Ones, that talks about your business and work, give advice and tips that others can learn from, and tell of personal experiences which causes some kind of emotion for the viewer. We will offer a few tips that will help you with that.

1. Define your brand

Who are you? What's the person you want to present to the audience? Are you interested in offering tutorials, maybe you are a fitness instructor, marketing expert? Perhaps you're a freelance writer or graphic designer who can share interesting tidbits about what your typical workday is like or even inside tips and tricks to help someone interested in your field. Take their skills to the next level. Even a tedious office job will be a basis for your personal branding. You can publish videos about style, have tips and tricks that help people deal with deadlines and responsibilities, and sneak-peeks into your organization's culture.

Remember: this is not a channel for your business, so you won't be launching video ads through it. It is part of any personal branding attempt, therefore, you should invest your complete personality in it.

This will be the beginning point of your efforts: figure out what type of personal brand you're going to build. It should be based on your interests and profession. Remember: you will want people to see you as a professional when they Google your name. If you work in an up-tight business environment, for example, then filming fitness videos with almost no clothes on is not a good idea.

2. Set up the profile

What name are you going to choose for your channel? You can use your own name, but you can even come up with a cool channel name that grasps its essence. Here are a few more things to pay attention to when setting up the channel:

- Provide your bio in the About section and explain what this channel is about. Make sure it includes links to even your LinkedIn profile, Facebook, Twitter and Instagram pages, and your official website if you have one. Yes, you *should* have your own website if you're trying to build a brand around your name.
- Play with the settings. YouTube allows a person to make the latest video as the featured video on your channel. You can create the titles and tags for the channel, and you can customize the layout in a way that works for you.

3. Maintain a logical progression

You won't be publishing random videos on topics that come to your mind. Personal branding is a continuous process.

When you're focused on building your personal brand, consider consistency and logical progression constantly. Create many playlists and make sure to invite your subscribers and viewers to take a peek at other helpful videos after watching one of them. The more they see of you, the stronger the impression they will have of your personal brand.

4. It's all about branding

Writer Roberta Collins has explained that filming videos is not enough. "You need something to be recognized by. An intro is a must. If you take a look at some of the most popular channels on YouTube, like TED, for instance, you'll notice they start with a recognizable intro. Do the same thing for your videos. Needless to say, you should hire someone to edit the material in the most professional way if you do not possess the skills for that. You want short, snappy intros and videos that are right on the money."

Along with the introduction, you will need more details to help you to build your personal brand through YouTube videos. Your branding style is very important. The way you talk and the humor you use, the unusual topics you cover... all these things are part of your brand. Think of an unusual twist that makes you different from the competition.

5. Be consistent!

People won't subscribe to your channel because of a single video. They want to see even more content, so they will know you have so many amazing things to offer. Then, YouTube will continue suggesting your latest videos to all subscribers, so you'll have a constant audience that's counting on you to entertain them.

Make a video publishing schedule and stay true to it. The more content you provide, the stronger your personal brand becomes.

Filming videos can be scary. It's like revealing your weakest points to a huge audience. However, it's also an incredible experience that places you in the forefront of an endless flow of feedback. Learn from it, and grow your personal brand into a digital empire, whether it's to help you land a new career, become a social media influencer or building a small business from scratch, whatever it is having a positive YouTube presence with a loyal viewership will go very far in helping you create a successful and lucrative personal brand.

In the section above, we discuss the importance of YouTube as a cornerstone for building a successful and lucrative personal brand, you can be proud of. However for the sake of convenience and those that prefer to have step-by-step instructions, below is a list containing 16 of the most important steps required to set up and maintain a successful YouTube presence. Then builds a substantial following within your given market demographic and/or viewership communities.

1. Profile branding

Your positioning on YouTube videos should first be decided. In case you already maintain a brand statement, you can continue applying the same position.

The web properties assist you with anything for branding your profile. There are channels that have various faces and for such categories, a topic or company name should be utilized for the company branding.

Your branding should use a complete name for channels that only possess one face. This is an aspect to be focused on as the channel is blocked from being altered later.

2. Choosing your YouTube name for your channel:

When choosing names for your channel, your name, illustration name or your business name can be employed.

Your own name can be utilized in case you want to brand yourself.

After registering, you will own a URL. The name can be picked depending upon the scheme that is to be posted.

3. Setting up a profile:

YouTube is a root where millions vie to catch other's attention, then filing the profile is important identical to other social media sites.

Try using a professional picture first that is everywhere. You are allowed to include a link that best showcases your personal brand which can be a blog or your LinkedIn profile.

4. Information about channels:

When YouTube is considered, there are plenty of accounts to be applied from and many persons do not know this fact.

If you're clued-up in the same section, opting for the "guru" account is favorable as custom logos are accepted and links are added.

5. Channel customization:

For customizing the channel, opening up the account and visioning it in this actual mode is to be achieved. With the screen open, the upper right-hand corner will be a tab called "switch to player mode".

While this step is completed, a fresh design of the page is obtained. In this manner, visitors can see the newest video of yours and others from the sidebar.

6. Latest video option:

For your audience to view your latest video, click the "edit" button in the top right corner of your screen. Here you will discover the "featured video" section. You can change this to the "use most recent" where your brand is established and your latest video is then made viewable when people click on your channel.

7. Themes and colors:

You can choose the themes and the color selection with the colors of your brand which are tied into your PowerPoints, websites, blogs or concern cards. Fonts and colors are then altered and your own background image can be utilized. There are free YouTube designs from a variety of websites that you can use as well.

8. Modules:

For you to develop your YouTube community, any recent activity, comments or even your friends are important options found in the modules section of your channel. These tabs will help a lot with your personal brand building.

9. Channel titles and tags:

Your YouTube channel titles and tags are the most important feature to focus on since they will be the terms that people will use to find your videos.

To do this, first click on 'edit channel' button and go to the 'settings' button. From there you will be allowed to create a title for your channel. The names of the tags you choose should be appropriate to the content of your videos. Let's say you do videos on flower arranging. The tags that would best suit your videos (depending on what flowers you were using for the videos) would be roses, flower arranging, stems or any other plant related terms.

10. Developing quality videos:

Content on YouTube is king and cultivating content that is worthy makes it more easy to spread around on the Internet. By making your video content interesting or funny will help you gain viewers and subscribers. There are many aspects that you need to concentrate on when filming the quality content.

When using video equipment that is employed for devising your videos, go for the ones with better clarity and more advanced if you want it to look proficient. To go for a more professional look, use lights, amplifiers, a sound system and more.

11. Remarkable content:

When filming a video, it is best to take multiple shots and then delete the shots that you do not think will work for the video. Also make sure the video is still in line with the theme and tags you had chosen to use along with the description of the video. With the description, add a link to your website where visitors to the video can click to take them to buy the product you are selling on YouTube.

12. Promoting videos to Facebook:

You can share the videos across all the social media platforms that you use such as your Facebook page. Facebook as a feature called the "YouTube video box application on Facebook" to add videos to your profile page and your "fan" page. You do not have to pay to use this feature.

13. Sharing process with other social media sites:

There are options that allow you to share your YouTube videos on Twitter and Google Reader as well. It is important that as a user, you should know your audience and then send the videos to your audience via these options.

14. Linking videos to your blog:

YouTube provides an easy way to add your videos to your blog. To do this, go to the settings and then click on the "blog setup" tab. This embeds your videos into your blog with the size measurements, borders, font styles, colors and many more functionalities.

15. Linking your videos everywhere:

As your brand builds up with more traffic as people view your videos, your ranking on YouTube should go up as you add more links to your videos. To do this, instigate a link from your resume to your YouTube channel or video, a link from your social media profiles, from your email signatures, or from your personal branding presentation.

16. The importance of Channel art:

Channel art showcases on many electronic devices so it is important to concentrate this aspect.

Using a font size of 14 makes your work readable and not too cluttered. Your channel art needs to focus on what you do, who you are and if you will post content in the future. To enhance visibility, your profile picture should also focus on what you are trying to communicate to the viewers.

Final thoughts:

When building your personal brand, it is necessary to show your skills, values, passion, and other personality traits you possess that way your brand differs from all the others on YouTube while adding great video content. By keeping the tips above in mind, you will be noticed amongst all the other million visitors.

There are billions of unique visitors to YouTube, where six billion hours of videos a month are watched, and where every minute there are nearly one hundred hours of videos uploaded. This chapter is an opportunity for you to become associated with others and to connect faster as a brand with customers.

Chapter 3: Facebook

It is difficult trying to ignore Facebook's ability to be personal branding tool — and not because it is the largest of all the social media platforms. What is more imperative is Facebook has always been well designed to share information, words, videos, website links, photos, and more to help you tell your story in ways that both inform and entertain people. Let us not forget that today everyone carries it around in their pocket. Facebook is on smartphones and people check their messages and favorite their and everyone else's page status at least three to four hours per day. According to a recent study's results, if you want to launch a personal brand within a given market demographic or community, then having a well thought out and completed Facebook page is a definite must for your personal brand.

Facebook, and abilities to simultaneously switch between the written word, photos, videos and websites (not to mention its new streaming features) allows you to expertly maintain the gentle balance of socializing and interacting with your chosen community and/or

market demographic, while also sharing enough of your personal brand , so that your followers get a good representation what others experience when they meet you in person.

Your reputation forms on Facebook in ways similar to how it forms in any community, online or otherwise. It's based on what others know about you — firsthand and inferred. Your reputation includes: (it's also important to remember that. Just like in real life. It takes a lifetime to build a reputation in the second loses. But I might realize, the more popular your Facebook or any other social media platform for that matter, the easier it is for people to find your brand and provide you with us. In other words, the more popular you are and/or positive reputation. You have the better your personal brand will duel for the long-term.)

Ways you behave generally
People you associate with
Information you share
Information others share

Looking at this list, you can see that you can't completely control your reputation on Facebook. Be careful who you hang out with. (Just like in real life. The people who make friends with on Facebook can have a very positive or very negative effect on your brand in a matter of seconds to select those friend invites wisely)

Whether you plan to use Facebook for business or not, it's a good idea to take some defensive measures to protect your personal brand. One of the best steps is to take advantage of what Facebook calls notifications: notices sent to your personal e-mail inbox or via text message based on actions by others on Facebook.

Consider your big-picture strategy

Your Facebook profile has lots of content areas to share optional personal information, a nod to Facebook's legacy as a college social networking site. Before deciding what to share, ask yourself basic networking questions:

What do I need to share to showcase my personal brand?

What other information am I willing to share?

What should I keep private — or not share at all?

Your answers determine what really belongs in your profile and suggest a general framework for your Facebook behavior, including ongoing content sharing and privacy-setting strategies.

Optimize what everyone can see

Everyone, including the online public, can see four things about your Facebook account:

The name at the top of your Facebook profile

Your Facebook custom username/account URL

Your current profile picture

Your Facebook Timeline cover photo

Making this information public is Facebook's way of making it easier for people to find you on Facebook. Consider customizing all four to your advantage:

Recognizable name: Facebook makes you use your real name to set up your account but gives you flexibility when it comes to the name that shows at the top of your profile. Use a nickname if it helps you be more recognizable and better matches your brand.

Unique username: With so many people on Facebook, getting your first choice may be difficult. Be creative in thinking of alternatives, but remember that you may want to add this URL to your business card and e-mail signature. The username has to make sense for your personal brand.

Public profile photo: This photo falls outside of any privacy settings, meaning anyone can view it. Therefore, choose one that is both friendly and professional.

Facebook Timeline cover photo: Facebook users are encouraged to upload a cover photo that serves as an 851-x-315-dpi header of their Timeline. Consider uploading an image that helps showcase your personal brand. Just remember, it's public.

Decide on your privacy settings

How widely you share other information you add to Facebook — profile elements, updates, comments, photos, and more — is up to you. Your first level of control is in deciding whether you post that information on Facebook in the first place!

You can also use privacy settings to manage which content posted by others can link (tag) directly back to your Facebook profile. Just know this: Preventing tagging doesn't stop someone from posting that content. The content is still on Facebook where it was originally posted. It's just harder for your network to connect that it relates to you.

Populate your Facebook profile

With your brand-awareness strategy in mind, purposefully complete your Facebook profile to include information such as the following:

Your work experience
Your educational experience
Links to your LinkedIn profile, website, blog, Twitter account, YouTube channel, and other sites
You may consider leaving blank (or limiting views to) personal information, such as relationship status,

religion, and political affiliation. Of course, there are exceptions to this guideline. For example, a political candidate would likely want to include information about his political views on the profile.

If you have your own Facebook page for your business, link it to your work experience entry so that your personal network can easily join you there as well.

The About Me section is your opportunity to tell your personal brand story in a more direct manner. Let your readers know what you do, as well as why you do what you do — your passion for the business. As with all things online, use keywords that resonate with your readers.

Share your personal brand story one post at a time

After you've set up your Facebook profile to showcase your personal brand and added Facebook connections, you can work toward building better relationships with those connections. You do so by posting content consistent with your personal brand and participating in related conversations started by others, either on other personal Facebook profiles, in Facebook Groups, or on Facebook Pages.

People notice not only what you post but how you post it. Be sure to proofread everything you write before posting. Don't write important posts when you're tired, upset, or overly emotional (whether happy or otherwise).

Below is a step-by-step guide to Facebook annual personal brand:

1. Choose your strategy:

Choosing your goals to build your branding strategy upon is a wise decision. However, there may be several ways to reach the goals you have chosen but not all of them are the right choices. That is where you need to wisely and carefully choose your plans by first deciding what you want your brand to depict and who your target audience is.

Next, distinguish your skills and capabilities, then decide how you can go about your strategy. You might not be the greatest in the branding business but you will learn how by your actions as per your strategy. Choosing the right strategies is the first step in branding yourself on Facebook.

2. Choose the right username for yourself:

Never choose a username that no one will remember or one that is hard to pronounce. Choose one that is handy and simple to remember.

Always select an exceptional username to use on all your social media profiles, not just Facebook. Your username will help Facebook users recognize you as a brand and to help you achieve your chosen brand name. Choose a username that is creative, not generic and use it on your website(s), email signature(s) and business cards.

3. Pay close attention to your profile photo and timeline cover photo:

Your profile photo and timeline cover photo need to represent your brand. After all, these are the smallest, most important details you need to show consideration for. Your photos should be as unique as your brand and username. You can either design your own or hire someone else to design your photos for those areas. This will help your followers recognize you as your brand.

4. Clear and detailed profile information:

The key to a successful brand is a detailed and complete profile section. A user will look at your profile information first before moving onto another section of your brand profile. After all, your profile information tells about your brand and its origin story. Make sure keep the information complete and specific so users can understand about your brand and know what it is all about. To maintain a clearing in sites message all the way through the profile is important not to talk about things that are not positively impactful to your brand when building your personal brand page. More often than not, people have a propensity to treat their brand page like a personal page by rambling on about things that do not have anything to do with their brand. This is distracting to your followers in your chosen community.

5. Set privacy settings:

By choosing the contents you will make public, you are controlling the settings for your Facebook privacy no matter if it is your status, comments, tags, or photos. If you do not want yourself to be tagged in any other person's photos, then you can control the privacy settings on the tags.

However, your privacy settings are often overlooked when building your personal brand. People forget that just because it is a personal page that they do not have to mess with the settings. However, there are things you may not want to be recognized for. If so then it is a great idea to read up on the privacy settings to decide which settings to use that help your personal brand the best.

6. Share your brand story:

Make sure to share the story of how your brand came to be. People do want to hear how you got started as a brand and what you have done so far to partially achieve a full all powerful brand. Make sure to share your experiences and why you choose your brand so people become familiar with it and to understand it better. It will bring them closer to your brand and wind up following it.

7. Growing your network:

Try expanding your brand's network by retrieving contacts from other social media platforms. You can send your followers updates about your brand through an email list and by offering them updates through your Facebook profile. The same thing can be done through importing your contacts from other places such as your phonebook and instant messages.

Facebook features a tool that integrates your friends into the brand and posting updates on their walls . This feature is known as Facebook Connect.

8. Constant status updates:

Make sure to share your status updates regularly. If you do not post anything for months or weeks at a time, then you will begin to lose what followers you had and any you might have gotten recently. Continue to share information about your new, upcoming projects or any contest that you might organize. Engaging your followers with interesting updates will compel them to join the conversation.

9. Focus on your quality:

It is not the quantity of your work but rather the quality of it. Constant updates do not mean you should post worthless contents to make people aware of your existence as a brand.

Boring content will cause your followers to "unfollow" you so be sensitive about your updates. Always focus on quality content. Post something that is interesting to your readers and keeps them captivated.

10. Show off your skills:

Always display your skills and expertise for people to know who you are and what you can do.

If you are a web designer, then you can exhibit your successful projects and what your client had said about it. You can even add a link to your portfolio page that showcases more of your works.

Sharing your LinkedIn page on Facebook is a great way to show more of your skills to help you find new leads for your personal brand.

11. Create a group or page:

Create a group of people who are interested in your brand and continue added members as your brand grows. Starting a group discussion will keep your followers engrossed while you share more of your content. These groups can be public or private, depending on the discussions held within the group.

You can even target certain people from a precise industry to promote your brand and by sharing your brand page with a specific list of groups that is relevant to your business. This will help grow your network and help you meet new contacts and potential followers.

12. Organize events in your area:

Try organizing events in your area that are applicable to your brand. Become involved in a community to begin the event.

Because of this, you will discover new potential followers and meet new audiences carrying an equal interest in your brand class and supporting you.

These events are announced using Facebook events that share the date, venue and time of the occasion. Your followers and any others who would like to attend can

RSVP through the Facebook events calendar and you can give them more details about the function. If any changes are made then those who had RSVP'd can change their plans accordingly through the events page.

13. Promote, promote and promote some more:

Try to avoid boring your followers if you keep using the same updates as the ones before. Persistence might be key but using the same updates is almost spamming (we will go over this next). Try rewriting the updates to where they capture the readers' attention each time.

Promoting constantly in groups and pages that are relevant to your brand, is okay but again, spamming is not allowed. Make sure to write every time in an exciting way so people will understand your creativity and the difference your brand will make in their lives.

14. NO SPAMMING!:

Facebook is always filled with spammers. Spammers are people who post the same thing over again but with different URLs. When it comes to spammers, Facebook is one of the major target places for spamming. You will always find some content containing computer viruses in your timeline or links you do not recognize in between comments and conversations.

Always promote, never spam. Spamming is not a good way to attract attention to your brand. It clutters up Facebook and your pages to the point that no one wants to follow you anymore. Spamming only annoys your market demographic, viewers or community readers. If they do not click on it the first time, what makes you think they will click on it the second or one millionth time? The only thing that will happen is they will report you to Facebook and you could lose everything you had built while online.

15. Start discussions:

By posting interesting topics for discussions will coerce users into commenting and joining the conversations. Make sure to start these discussions within the group that directly relates to your brand. Discussions will help others learn new things about what they did not know and to share something that makes sense to them thereby allowing everyone who reads it to learn something new. Always seek out related topics and become absorbed in the conversation.

Starting a discussion will allow your chosen community to get to know you and your brand on a more personal level while helping your brand become connected with your target audience, or market demographic.

16. Engage with any and all networks:

Become engaged not only in groups but individually with people who are linked to your brand as well. You should greet your members often during groups discussions, Facebook events, contests and any time you log into the site. It helps with being courteous to them and impresses them with your politeness. It will also develop your professional relationship with them and might get you some neat deals later on. Engaging with your members will help you find updates on other markets and to learn something new yourself.

17. Start and run contests:

Contests are a great way to get your followers engrossed in your brand and they will continue to look for more contests to participate in on your page. Have contests either weekly, monthly or daily if you want.

Offering impressive prizes to winners and runners up will keep them interested in participating in upcoming contests. You can even promote those contests from your Twitter, LinkedIn, Reddit or other social media site for more results.

Besides attracting more viewers or readers in your market demographic, having a contest is a pleasant way to become involved in your chosen market demographic and give something back. This will also increase your readership, however, it is extremely important to keep your word when it comes to the contests. Do not be late in giving the prizes away and also do not be dishonest by offering the prize and then telling them that there was no prize to begin with.

18. Learn from brands that are bigger than yours:

Bigger brands are always on Facebook using it as their promotion and marketing tool. You just have to know where to find them. When you do, follow them and learn from their ideas on how they became successful. Study them every day to better understand their strategies and utilizing those strategies in your own brand promotion. It will offer you a chance to tryout the strategies and to learn the right and wrong ways to endorse a product. However, do not to deliberately copy their marketing strategies. You could run into some legal problems which will defeat the purpose of creating your personal brand. The best way is to take the crux of a favorite marketing strategy, and put your unique twist on it that shows off your personality. Just because they say, "Imitation is the sincerest form of flattery.", remember to not out-right copy them.

Conclusion:

Now you know Facebook has the power to aid you in branding yourself and in building a personal brand. Unlike other social media websites, Facebook provides a huge amount of options you can use and is a very adaptable way to market your product.

By learning from the major brands on how they have marketed the brands on Facebook and other social media sites, you can learn how to market your brand when using their tips. If you are establishing your own brand for the first time, start using Facebook today for more definite outcomes. However, while it is a good idea to study your favorite brands and influencers on social media to see what is working for attracting and keeping the attention of the viewers or readers in a given market demographic and/or online community, it is important to remember not to blatantly steal a copy a given market strategy for two reasons. One being, you will probably get sued by whoever owns the copyright and/or marketing campaign and two, if something is popular, and already being done and is less likely for a nether marketing campaign. The best thing to do is take the essence from a favorite marketing campaign and put a twist on it to show off your own unique character or personality.

Chapter 4: LinkedIn

It does not matter if you had intended to create it but you do own a personal brand if you have a social imprint online. You will need to enhance your personal brand, whether you are a freelancer or an entrepreneur just to survive in this day and age. If you have a powerful brand, then you can represent yourself as a trustworthy expert in your field of expertise.

Individuals and big brands use social media as a renowned way to increase and endorse their personal brands. LinkedIn is one of the most authoritative social media platforms intended to promote personal brands today.

Why use LinkedIn as a powerful personal branding tool?

LinkedIn is the unsurpassed business professional social media channel ever. It has turned out to be the greatest tool for personal branding and is guilty of being that way because consumers have always preferred to deal with a live person rather than a corporation.

With the human aspect, LinkedIn permits you to grow and interact with a more vastly targeted audience. By knowing your audience's demographics and background experiences, you can then create content that is engaging while launching your credibility online. There are a few ways to control LinkedIn as a powerful personal branding tool.

1. Building a Community

To begin, you need to build a community of specialists who respect your field of interest. With LinkedIn, you can find professionals easily who relate to your business and expand your professional network or you can try reaching out to others whom you believe will be able to help your business and your personal brand grow.

Sharing contents related to your targeted network's interest allows you to improve situations and thereby strengthen the relationship between you and your targeted audience.

2. Connecting with Potential Clients

Another benefit to building strong relationships is to generate sales. The more you enhance your relationship with your targeted clients, then the more likely they will buy from you. This straightforward strategy will increase your personal brand as well as any sales you will make. LinkedIn is an extraordinary way to help you reach out to your targeted audience, connecting with them to build-up your relationship online.

3. Reaching out to Journalists and Editors

No more than ninety-two percent of journalists for magazines, newspapers, radio and television are on LinkedIn. There are chances you could be published in one of those magazines or newspapers if you contact one of them. Discover those journalists who relate to your industry and try connecting with them and building relationships. It is better to prepare a list of any publications that directly deal with your niche and contact the writers of those publications while on LinkedIn.

4. Visiting LinkedIn Local Meetups

LinkedIn has a section for people to meet known as LinkedIn Local Meetups. Through LinkedIn local meetups, people go from online conversations to meetings offline through messages exchanged in real time and being present for LinkedIn local meetups to connect with like-minded people within or outside of your industry.

5. Letting the Professionals find you

Professionals also connect through LinkedIn and can contact you as well as you contacting them. Journalists, for example, can contact you for interviews or for an opportunity to speak. These opportunities will then help boost your personal brand. By optimizing your profile on LinkedIn, you can decide which keywords to use that are right for you while showing a clarity about who you are as a brand.

How do you go about building your LinkedIn profile to get results?

Here are a few ways to build your profile to get the best results for your brand.

A. Expressing Your Brand

Once a person's brand statement has been established, completed LinkedIn profiles usually rank within the top three results on Google searches. By having a complete, convincing profile is a remarkable way to control what others will see when searching for your brand while online.

B. Your Headline

Make sure to use all of your profile's space wisely, beginning with your headline to get the most from your LinkedIn profile.

First, your headline should be more than your job description. If you are in international development, make sure to be more specific about whether you are on a quest to make clean water accessibility a certainty in a third-world country or if your focus is in disaster relief. Make Your headline should be as compelling as possible. In fact, if your brand statement makes sense to use then use it!

C. Your Summary

Your summary is all the details about your brand. Refine what you have learned about yourself, including:

- ❖ Your key values
- ❖ Your strengths

- ❖ Your passions
- ❖ Your opinions
- ❖ and your personality

Be sure to talk about what makes you, you (or your one-line brand statement) and support that statement with goals that showcase your passion and key exploits that reflect your skills. Think about this as relating where you came from and where you are going as a brand. After all, you are telling your story.

Do not be afraid to let your personality's shine show itself to the world. Make sure to leave some fraction of your content for more personal elements which help you stand out as you spend most of the content on your professional profile as well.

If sustainability is the core value of your profile, or if you are fluent in three languages and have faith in the value of worldwide experiences, then make sure to include these details. It is alright to be opinionated about any issues in your field. Do not be fanatical (it never makes you any friends—or gets you any job offers), but you should know people are more interested in you if you have a genuine point of view.

Finally, if your name is usually misspelled, maybe consider inserting alternates in your summary, just in case. For example, if your name is Jackey Lewis, then include a little line at the bottom labeled, "Common misspellings: Jackie Lewis, Jackey Louis."

D. Your Experience

The experience section is a bigger, better, and more engaging version of your resume or a place to share what you have accomplished and just how well you have accomplished it.

The most important thing to consider is to highlight the duties that are aligned with your brand. For instance, if you are an editorial assistant, but have picked up some design work for your employer and understood that is the direction you want to move in, you will then want to focus on that experience throughout the experience section of your profile.

There is no one-page limit on LinkedIn to hold you back. A neat trick to try is to break down your position into multiple positions, particularly if you have very different responsibilities within the same role. Do not go nuts and add ten different descriptions for everything you have done before, but two or three descriptions that represent larger duties is acceptable.

One other huge difference between the experience section and your resume is your ability to assimilate multimedia. For every position, you should include your work on blog posts, SlideShare, and other media you might use for your brand. Be sure to be extra considerate of what media you will share and how it does connect to your brand. Pictures are the most attention-grabbing portion of your profile, so make sure you are highlighting on-message content.

E. Endorsements and Recommendations

How easy it is to get recommendations and endorsements is one of LinkedIn's greatest features. It makes obtaining authentication for your know-how forthright—and of course, the more buy-in you get from others, the easier it is to obtain new buy-in.

For endorsements, add about ten skills that best reflect the skills and experiences you want to be best known for. Remove any off-brand endorsements (for example, if your first job was in finance but you are focused on building your business expansion career now, you might not want to be listed as "accounting"). If at all possible, you need to rearrange your endorsements in an order that best aligns with your brand.

The swiftest way to get endorsements? Give them out! This ideal goes for recommendations as well. You can ask people directly to recommend you by sending a straightforward note letting a few of your key contacts know you are searching for a job or trying to build up your knowledge, and enquire if they would highlight a precise (on-brand) part of your background in their recommendation.

F. The Finishing Touches

The last thing to do before finishing up, modify your LinkedIn URL (Uniform Resource Locator) (to your name, or your name plus your field, if you have a conventional name) and connect with a few targeted groups in your area of expertise or industry.

As a side note: If there are LinkedIn groups you want to join but are offline, then turn off the group logo under the "group settings" tab. They will not show on your profile, but you will still have access to them.

Make sure to follow pertinent news that shows up through LinkedIn channels and influencers, as well as other companies. Stay on top of what is taking place and, even better still, share what you have learned along the way! You will show those who view your profile that you are well-informed about trends and current events in your area of expertise by frequently publishing links to stimulating articles, thoughts on what is going on in your industry, or even your work.

Last of all, know you can rearrange the sections of your profile if it makes logical sense for your brand. The summary section will always be on top, but you can move the publication section higher or your education lower, dependent on what is most relevant to you now.

Also remember to revise your profile in private. You can turn off the updates under the privacy settings tab, so you are not announcing every little tweak you make.

Wow! When your polished creation is complete, check to see if your LinkedIn profile conveys the statement of your brand. However, you might continue tweaking your profile even after you receive feedback.

And, despite how seamless it is this time around, you will want to continue revising it to ensure it stays current. In the end, the main point is to ensure hiring managers and recruiters are viewing the most innovative and greatest you out there.

1. Share notable news, advice and tips

Always make sure to share your status updates because your profile's visibility on LinkedIn will skyrocket the more you share your updates. You can even build your brand up gradually and earn the respect you deserve from your network of people if you either act as liaison for people on LinkedIn or if you share any and all beneficial tips and information. However, never spam (use the same message over with a different URL) your network of people is you continue to share just to share something only you though was interesting. It is better to provide some information than to overshare that information.

2. Sharing your opinions and starting discussions is the way to go on LinkedIn

You know it is time to take your brand further on LinkedIn when you feel confident about sharing the news and information, not to mention any tips and tricks you know, to shake things up on LinkedIn.

Sharing guarantees that you will gain "shares" and "likes" but if you want your brand and its visibility to grow, then you should be asking for "comments" instead. You do want to be seen as an expert in your chosen field of study on LinkedIn, right? For this to happen, you need to share your opinions on a variety of subjects and any questions you need answered while creating your status updates on LinkedIn.

If you do have an opinion, make sure it is polite and allows for readers to provide feedback through engrossing questions that asks for a response from those reading it and through precise calls to action. They might not agree with your opinion but then not every has the same ideas as you . Just make sure not to provoke them into hating you.

3. Follow thought leaders and/or companies and respond to them if they have questions for you.

When you follow and respond to things (status updates and articles) from companies and those thought of as thought leaders of your field or brand then you can become more visible on LinkedIn.

Every comment you make shows on your profile and any status updates on your contacts' home pages on

LinkedIn. Notable comments spark discussions and grow your visibility, your network of followers and your personal brand.

4. Recommendations for other members' skills and expertise are the best.

Even though they say "it is better to give than receive", we all love to receive rewards for our good deeds of giving to those who need it the most. By recommending the abilities and know-how of the people in your network, you will increase your LinkedIn popularity and the number of places that you profile shows up on. Plus, the more people often see your profile, the more you are likely to cultivate your network and to hear about fascinating prospects.

5. Make sure you participate in groups on LinkedIn or even start some groups

After talking about how to grow your visibility on LinkedIn, it is now time to talk about how to grow your network beyond its bounds. This is done by joining or creating as the case might be, LinkedIn Groups!

To make full use of these groups, the golden rule is to always add value. LinkedIn groups are not for spamming (mentioned earlier and throughout the book) or for dropping links to your blog post wherever you decide to drop them.

LinkedIn groups help others with what they need and they also begin discussions that are thought-provoking to add value to any groups you decide to join. By sharing links to useful information that someone else might need to know and adding a link to your website or blog every now and then is greatly appreciated by the group. There are at least five steps to take in order to join a LinkedIn group:

1. Find and submit an application for membership with stimulating groups

You can categorize thought-provoking groups by inserting specific keywords in the search box on top of your LinkedIn home page, or by skimming through the groups listed on LinkedIn profiles that bear a resemblance to your pursuits.

2. Always listen to the LinkedIn group

If the group has accepted you a member (group managers can choose to allow or reject access), take time to learn the dynamics of the group for a week or so.

What type of data is shared? What is the group's tone of voice? Who in the group are the top influencers? Attempt to grasp the big picture and to understand the rules of conduct for the group.

3. Reply to other members of the group

If you have studied the changing aspects of a LinkedIn group, you can begin to help others by contributing in discussions. You must be patient, however. You might have to still earn your way into the group. You need to add quality to the discussion and try not to excessively aggravate others.

4. Share any information and start any discussions about anything

After a bit (the exact time frame depends on your pledge and/or the groups' dynamics), you can begin to share your information, questions, opinions, tips, and tricks. In other words: you should start discussions of your own. If you do this, make sure keep it super short and add clear questions or calls to action to request advice from the group.

5. Stay committed and focused within the group

Now is the time to merge your position in the group, reaping the profits from your efforts and to assist others wherever you can. Stay dedicated and attentive on your topic. The more you share and provide, the greater your brand will be and the more people will connect, talk, meet, and work with you. LinkedIn groups are where chances will find you instead.

Be sure to remember these ten mistakes to avoid with LinkedIn.

1. Do not use anything other than a professional looking photo

You should never use a photo of you drinking in public, vacationing at the beach or messing around with friends. LinkedIn is a social media platform that strives for a professional look. These types of photos are more reserved for Facebook and Twitter than LinkedIn. The best picture for LinkedIn is one of preferably your head and shoulders. People want to see what you look like so always use a professional-looking photo rather than a goofy selfie.

2. Never lie on your profile.

It would be embarrassing if one of your contacts had discovered a lie on your profile. It is best to be honest when creating your profile so you will not be kicked off the site. After all, every one of your connections can see your profile.

3. Do not use LinkedIn's default text

If you use the default text that LinkedIn provides, then you are making yourself as uninteresting as the font style. You want to be unique not bland. You want to add your personal touch to the words used on LinkedIn when contacting those you meet on the website.

4. Avoid using the "Friend" option on LinkedIn

If you do not know the professionals you talk to on LinkedIn, naming them as a friend is a major faux pas. Not only that, those same professionals are annoyed at you which is not conducive to a good work relationship.

5. Never forget including all your external links

If you have a presence on Twitter or Facebook or if you have a personal brand website, adding a link to your profiles on those sites is a good idea. While LinkedIn is a professional social media website, people want to know who you are personally as well as professionally. Interesting fact: You can add up to three links under the "Websites" heading on your profile. There is even another section to incorporate your Twitter account (three links for this section as well).

6. Do not leave your LinkedIn profile incomplete

If you do not know if your profile is complete, LinkedIn can help with its "wizard" to guide you step by step in creating your profile. It will help you format your Heading, Summary, Experience and Skills and Expertise sections. These sections should be "keyword rich".

7. Do not get lazy when sharing updates and links.

Always modify your messages on LinkedIn. Do not use the same messages that you use of Twitter or Facebook. It is annoying to everyone when they look at the hashtags and @ Twitter handles on LinkedIn messages and status updates. (Side note: Clicking on Twitter handles will send you to the person's Twitter page and clicking on the hashtag will send you to where you can look up whatever topic has the hashtag attached to it.) Make sure to take a few minutes and personalize your updates and links to obtain the profits.

8. Using LinkedIn groups purely for getting "linkbacks" to your website or blog is never good.

If you do this, it is considered spamming. Spamming is a way to get you kicked off LinkedIn. Spamming is using the same message over again using a different URL. Spamming clutters up the site and annoys the hell out of people. A LinkedIn group that is well-managed is also closely scrutinized and most will only allow discussions, commentary and questions. Some will even permit you to add a link to other people's blog posts, which is strange since they will not allow you to add a link to your own blog. Even if your post is totally relevant to the discussion; it is perceived as self-promotion.

9. NEVER EVER spam your connections.

LinkedIn is not an email marketing platform to spam others with any events or news from your company or brand! As mentioned above, spamming is annoying, not to mention illegal on websites.

10. People who DO NOT know you should never be told to write any recommendations for you.

If you do not know someone on LinkedIn, then they do not know you. Asking if they can recommend you to someone is awkward, to say the least and you will not get a recommendation if you pester them for one.

Chapter 5: Twitter

Seems like everyone is on Twitter these days. Used to be everyone was on MySpace and Facebook when they wanted to get together and converse while online. It is shocking to know that even the current President is on Twitter 24/7.

But what you might not know is that you can promote yourself as a freelancer, entrepreneur and businessperson while on Twitter. That's right! You can create a personal brand using Twitter. In this chapter, we will go over the ten ways you can build a personal brand on Twitter.

First, perfect your Twitter profile.

This first part is the easiest. To improve on your Twitter profile, you must:

► Use a photo of your face instead of the logo you use for your company

► Have a concise image of what you do as per your brand

► Use an engaging cover photo that exemplifies you and your brand

▶ Make sure to add links relevant to who you are as a brand such as LinkedIn and Facebook

▶ Create a biography on Twitter that is strong and flatters you (humorous or otherwise)

▶ and Provide a link to your blog if you have one

It is best if your picture is up-to-date and consistent on all the social media sites you use, not just on Twitter.

Second, make sure to log in and do something each day.

By posting something every day, you guarantee that you are seen as well as heard. Each post you make will make people want to talk to you and maybe hire you for a job. This also ensures that people will follow you on Twitter. If you have been a member of Twitter for years, then only taking a few minutes out of the day to engage your followers is recommended. You can also space out the spreading of your content as you go along. The more persistent you are, it will not be long before you get over a thousand followers who will then invite others to follow you.

It sometimes helps to schedule out your Twitter time so you do not overwhelm yourself with posts and replying to posts from others you follow. Staying active on Twitter will help your brand grow when others notice you and your brand. There are many on Twitter who do just that but there are too many to count and to name within this chapter.

Thirdly, follow those who have more experience promoting their brands on Twitter

As they say, "It's not what you know, but who you know." It basically means that if you know a person who promotes themselves on social media, then it does not matter that you know your specific skills. All that matters is that there are others you could be learning from while growing your brand via Twitter.

By following those who have grown their brand through Twitter, you can learn more skills than you would have learned going it alone. Make a list of those who have been successful that you can contact by:

- ❑ Responding to their tweets they have posted
- ❑ Retweeting those posts
- ❑ Help them if they ask for your help
- ❑ Greeting them when you log on

❑ Follow them on other social media websites such as Facebook or Instagram.

On Instagram, the messages are more personal than other websites. Sometimes they will share a personal post on Instagram and then tweet a message about the personal Instagram message. You can then ask them a question about the post because you already know what is going on because you followed them on Instagram.

Let's say you have been following one of the brand leaders you have been talking to on Twitter while on Instagram. They post a picture on Instagram of them at a county fair in their hometown. Then a few days later, they tweet about their town's county fair. You can respond to them and then ask them how they enjoyed the fair. This adds a personal touch to the message and shows the person that you are interested in their life outside of their brand.

By doing this, they could help you come in contact with other experts in the industry thereby helping you to gain more experience in growing your brand. It comes in handy knowing who has excelled in their industry for it helps you grow as a brand.

Fourth, give value to your tweets to add context.

When you add context to your tweets, you are adding value to your brand while on Twitter. There are two ways you can provide value quickly: by sharing your post and by sharing the posts of others. Try finding a ratio for doing these two things. I am sure you will find it makes it easier to add the value to your brand and your posts about your brand.

Fifth, besides posting tweets about your brand, add personal posts as well.

That's right! Post some personal tweets. Many people do not want to share every aspect of their lives with perfect strangers but how else will you get them to buy your services through your brand if they do not know why you started your brand? Maybe something had changed in your life that caused you to want to start your own brand. Wouldn't you want to share that?

You want people to care about your brand not to feel swamped with serious things. Post some personal pictures with you surrounded by friends or family. Maybe have a few posts that have pictures of you in the garden or wearing a favorite outfit. All these things add a personal touch that helps you connect with others without feeling robotic. These people are supposed to care about you because it adds a human element to your brand and makes you more memorable.

Sixth, become a part of any Twitter chatrooms.

Twitter chatrooms are essential to growing your brand. Those that you meet in these chatrooms are some of the greatest people you can meet and chat with. These people are sincere and they are always active on Twitter. Even if your brand is completely grown to your satisfaction, you can still connect with these people because they will help you should you need it. These chatrooms are tight-knit communities and like a community, they are always willing to help out when you are in need.

There are a few Twitter chatrooms that might be useful to you as you grow your brand. These include:

- ❖ #Mediachat
- ❖ #Twittersmarter
- ❖ and #CustServ

These groups help you add value to your brand especially once you are invited to be a guest on a chat. This boosts your credibility as a brand instantly.

Seventh, most definitely follow those who are actively on Twitter.

Active people on Twitter are your best friends. By following them, you can gain followers because active people share tweets and engage with you often enough to make others want to follow you as well.

Following people works a few years ago and it still works today.

Eighth, create a blog or link one on Twitter.

A blog will help you immensely with your brand on Twitter. It will allow people to learn more about you as an entrepreneur and it will help your brand grow because of this. Twitter is perfect for adding short content, interacting with people and letting your voice be heard. A blog, on the other hand, will take that to a whole other level. It helps to showcase your brand to help you gain even more followers than before. Twitter is basically the voice in which your thoughts can be heard through your blog.

Ninth, take full advantage of videos on Twitter.

Twitter videos work very well when growing your brand. Those who take the time to make the videos and using them as posts have taken advantage of this method thereby standing out on Twitter. A good example of this comes from @PTwyford. He has taken advantage of this method so that people know him personally through his videos and so he has more followers.

Tenth, brag, brag, and brag some more!

If you have been interviewed for an article, been named an expert in your chosen field, tried something that worked, saw any rewards from your brand or were even listed by someone else as a person to follow on Twitter, do not hesitate to brag about those accomplishments. This will boost your brand to new heights. You want your followers to know what you have accomplished since starting out. It adds context to your brand and shows that you are an expert in something besides being the least annoying sibling.

Most people do not do this for they fear they will be branded as conceited. These people then become unnoticeable and start to lose followers rather than gain them.

Last but not least eleventh, be yourself!

If someone tells you that you need to be professional while promoting your brand on Twitter, don't listen to them unless you are a person with a professional attitude. Be yourself and not what someone else want you to be. If you are not genuine, then everyone will take you at face value.

The same goes for your shared content as well. Be yourself! Share personal photos, favorite quotes or jokes you have heard that you think others might like to hear.

Conclusion to building your Twitter brand:

Take this advice and learn it, live it, and love it!

Chapter 6: Personal Brand Website

The number one networking tool you can use to sell your brand is not a resume but rather a website that extols the virtues of your brand and your skills. Your resume is always the same as everyone else's, the same font, the same pictureless features, and the same format. It is enough to make you want to not find any work because it is not personal and unique to you.

After all, a resume becomes old instantly and you need to rewrite it each time you want to apply for jobs. That is where a personal brand website comes into play.

There are four reasons why you should have a personal brand website:

1) A website is much easier to change than a resume. You do not need to create a website from scratch each time something changes. You just have to change the parts that are outmoded to better suit the ever-changing business world.

2) A website makes it easier for someone to find you without having to go through your Facebook or Twitter account. Sometimes you can even

have a resume on your website. Through your website, you can gain more clients and gain interviews for job offers as well.

3) A website makes you stand out in a crowd of other people seeking work. You can tell everyone who visits your website about what you have accomplished and any skills you have that are different from others in the same field of expertise as you.

4) Building a website will help you gain more skills such as optimization and customization. Learning these skills will boost your level of expertise. Letting a potential client know that you know your way around the net will make them want to hire you instead of your competition, especially if said client owns an advertising company.

Creating a personal brand website takes at least five steps to make your personal brand website dreams come true.

Step 1. **You need to obtain a domain name.**

There are quite a few website-builder sites you can use to gain a domain name such as GoDaddy.com,

WordPress.com and Wix.com. However, if you want your website to stand out, you usually have to pay an exorbitant fee to have your site permanently published until you can sell it to someone else for more money than you had paid for the website to begin with or you have to delete the site completely.

Though, if you do have that kind of cash on you, then there is nothing to worry about. Just make sure your domain name is not silly nonsense about maybe the title of a cartoon you used to watch. A safe solution is to use your first and last name.com. If your name is more common than you like, then throw your middle initial in the domain name as well. If that does not work, then maybe use a short play-on-words of your name before the .com. The domain extensions that work best are .com, .org, .me or .co. Never use .info or .biz.

Step 2: **If you are using WordPress, then you need to install it and start working on your website.**

While WordPress is used mostly for blogging, you can create a website that does not require you to create a blog. WordPress is self-hosted, making it easier for you to set up your website. Once your website is set up, then you can begin building it. WordPress will give you the option to freestyle your site or to allow WordPress to help you build your site by suggesting ideas.

With WordPress, there are two basic designs to choose from: one-page or multi-page. If your brand is small and you do not have a lot of information about your brand, then the one-page design works best. On the other hand, if your brand has tons of information about it, then the multi-page design is the way to go.

If you go with the multi-page design, make sure to include:

- ❖ An About Me page as your home page.
- ❖ A Biography page that has more details about you.
- ❖ A Resume page.
- ❖ A Contact page so people can talk with you about things on your website or to hire you for jobs.
- ❖ Other pages such as
  - ⊥ A Portfolio page with any works or writing you might have done.
  - ⊥ A Hire Me page for clients to hire you from.
  - ⊥ A Blog page.

- A Press page for any online newspaper clippings about your work or interview videos from a television station.
- An Impossible List with your goals laid out for others to see.

Step 3: **You need to choose a theme for your site.**

WordPress has thousands of themes to choose from. However, not all of them will be suited to your brand style. As a solution, there are four themes you can use that might work best: Simple, Verbosa, Lovecraft and Ultra.

Simple theme is your basic theme that is versatile, free and easy to use since it lets you customize your pages even more than any other theme. If you do not have a specific preference when it comes to themes then this is the design for you.

The Verbosa theme is much like the Simple theme in its easy customization capability. However, you cannot edit the structure of it like you can with the Simple theme.

The Lovecraft theme is mostly used by those who have created a blog instead of an entire website but it does have a clean menu, a huge image area to place any image that you want and great design layout.

Last but not least, the Ultra theme (created by Themify) is a premium theme that you have to pay for in order to use. However, it is the more flexible of all the themes. It has fifteen header styles, more colors, fonts and page layouts to choose from and a portfolio feature as well.

Step 4: **You need to add widgets and plugins to help improve your website even further.**

WordPress works with small or large code, known as plugins which provides more functionality to your personal brand website. With plugins, you do not have to download any .zip files which makes it easier to use without having to open the .zip file and extract the plugin from it. Here are a few essential plugins you will need:

- Ninja Forms
- WP Super Cache
- and UpdraftPlus

Widgets (elements that go on any part of your theme that has been set up to display said widgets) also help with the improvement of your website.

Step 5. **You can use other things to make your website better.**

There are a few things that can make your website even better than before. These include:

- Personal Website SEO (Search Engine Optimization)
- Upgrading how you think as time passes
- and Upgrading your site to better suit you and your brand

Now you are wondering where you can take your website from here. That's simple. Continue growing your brand and growing your personal brand website as well. This is but one stepping stone towards becoming recognized as a brand.

Chapter 7: Blog

Some say that blogging is a thing of the past. That is where they are wrong. Just because social media has taken over our daily lives does not mean that people have stopped blogging. There are many people who still blog like Neil Patel, Neil Gaiman, and others (mostly authors). The benefits of blogging for business are never-ending, but a strategic, research-based approach needs to be in place for the best results. The problem: You come across many suggestions on how to promote your brand through blogging without knowing how to execute a content marketing strategy.

We have good news. Knowing how to do just that is what this chapter is about. Here are the things you need to know about blogging and how to make it work for your brand.

Search Engine Optimization (SEO)

One of the ways you can drive traffic to your blog that is most beneficial is through search engine optimization (SEO) techniques. SEO is how to craft your content in such a way that it is easily ranked by major search engines like Google.

Imagine that a thousand people are searching for "cupcake delivery in St. Louis, Missouri." If you are one of three in the business of baking and delivering cupcakes in St. Louis, then being the first result in a search engine would increase your business substantially.

Blogging can help with these tactics in multiple ways:

- Keyword density
- Backlinking
- Frequent updates
- Long-tail keywords

Take some time to research each concepts and then begin implementing them into your blog's content regularly.

Establish Authority

You want to be known as an expert and thought leader to your audience and target market, right?

But why?

Because you want to be the first in mind when people are looking for the best roofer, or personal trainer that exists. A giant part of creating this perception entails publishing authoritative content that demonstrates your knowledge and expertise in any particularly given area.

Use Analytics

Analyzing the traffic patterns and most popular blog content is a necessity. Choose what your audience is already interested in, instead of randomly choosing topics to focus on. You don't want to talk about going to the supermarket if your brand deals with clothes, especially if you do not talk about buying clothes at said supermarket. However, you will want to put a twist on your content that speaks to your target customer.

Respond to Your Customers' Needs

After discovering what topics your customers are interesting in, then it is time to respond to that and any other needs your customers might want. Adding a forum for your customers to join if they have any questions or concerns about your brand is a great way to respond to what they need. If you do not want to add a forum to your blog's website, then adding a link to another forum site such as Quora or Reddit will also help you respond to your customers' needs. Take Regan Morton, for example. Morton is a digital specialist at the marketing firm FiG Advertising + Marketing in Colorado. In terms of pain points, "This is a great way to generate interesting content based on what your potential consumers are asking for."

Make the Most of Social Channels

Social media channels act as a form of blogging and are not only a way to promote your awesome blog content. While many people still read traditional blogs, the medium itself is changing all the time.

There are three ways many people and businesses now "blog" in different ways on diverse social media platforms:

- Microblogging on Twitter
- Vlogging on YouTube
- Photo blogging on Instagram

You want to have a strategy in place to meet your potential customers where they are already consuming content.

For example, Uwe Weinkauf, CEO of MW2 Consulting, an e-commerce consultancy, cites Zappos as an influential example of how using social media can improve a brand. They use Twitter to highlight fascinating facts about their brand and their newest additions. "What's more is that they do it in a helpful and funny way,"

Another fun part about social media is that it can be a two-way conversation. Not only are you relaying information in the places where your customers are showing up, but you can also engage in "social listening" for feedback that will improve the customer experience as well.

Create a Content Marketing Plan that works for You

Your business blog should always deliberately target topics and information your ideal client is looking for. Instead of being reactive, creating content whenever you feel like it, be proactive about producing your blog content.

A well-crafted content marketing plan will anticipate topics and time them in such a way to resonate with a target market. Creating a content calendar will help with this endeavor. For example, if you generate software for tax accountants, you will want to time content that coincides with several important tax deadlines.

For instance, Harrison Doan, the director of analytics at Saatva, a popular online mattress retailer, stresses the much needed importance of a well-planned content calendar. "An organized content calendar can make or break your company's blog. We use our content calendar to schedule regular blog posts, but we also include quite a few reminders for things like holidays, seasons, and major events for our business."

Shana Haynie is a creative director at Vulpine Interactive, a social media agency, cautions business owners who are wanting to incorporate blogging into their marketing strategy: "Ultimately, your content needs to be researched, planned, and exceedingly valuable to the people who you want to build a customer relationship with."

Implement Marketing Automation

After studying these suggestions, your head is possibly spinning at the prospect of doing these things plus doing them well for your business blog. Do not worry, you can find plenty of tools for developing a "set-it-and-forget-it" approach to your business blogging strategy.

These tools will help you to create and manage your content calendar and maybe even push it out to the countless social channels out there. Many of these tools offer free trials so you can examine what works the best for your business needs:

- Co-Schedule
- Meet Edgar
- HootSuite
- Dlvrit

Spreading your blog content around is only one piece of the puzzle. Be ready for when your audience has questions and demands more content. If this does happen, you can rest assured that you are on the right track.

Using blogs to market your business does not need to be painful or too overly complicated. Begin with a few tactics that you can manage and then move on to more once you have mastered those. If all goes according to plan, you should see your customer-base and revenues increase as a reward for your blogging efforts!

Chapter 8: Personal Branding, from A to Z

1) *Authenticity*

Building a brand around yourself and your personal image will require more deep thought it is not something that you are just going to jump into with both feet plug and play style, you really have to know what you want out of your personal brand because never forget. You're not selling a product like a vacuum cleaner or a laptop. You are selling yourself and/or your image or persona to the public hoping they will become fans, patrons or viewers.

In trying to decide just exactly what it is you want to accomplish with your brand, you are more likely to learn, a lot about what your strengths are and what your weaknesses are, what you value, who you are, and many other things. Embracing all the various aspects of your personality, your strengths, and weaknesses, your beliefs and values and goals are the keys to finding and understanding your authentic self, which will lead to building a meaningful, strong and long-lasting personal brand that will serve you and your fans and/or patrons well.

For many years when working to develop your personal brand, don't be afraid to tap into your emotions. And tapping into those special layers of your personality, those things that make you, unique.

2) *Bio/Biography*

A professional bio (biography) for yourself provides a clear and concise summary of your professional-background that represents you across many different mediums — such as social media, blog posts, a speaker profile, etc. think of your professional bio as a digital-first impression, just as with meeting someone in person for the first time. You get only one opportunity to make a first impression with your personal brand - if you don't get the attention of a customer or patrons in the first minute after they click on your profile. Then they'll more than likely to click to something else and forget about you. A minute later — this is why having a clear and concise biography to establish a good first impression plays such an important part, in the definition of your personal brand.

Problem is, most people do not keep it updated as often as they should.

A professional bio, that is short, is one of those things most people don't think about. That is until, suddenly, a person has been asked to shoot over via email, one's professional bio. And one has approximately one afternoon to come up with one. So, you must be constantly updating your bio with your skills. You have gained new experiences you have had, along with anything else that you think will speak directly to your chosen market demographic. It is important to not forget that. Aside from helping you to establish a good first impression with your potential market demographics, your professional biography is a digital representation of you and your brand. This is across all the many various social media platforms out there on the internet. Think of this as your digital reputation. It takes a lifetime to build a solid reputation and less than a second to lose it. So, your professional biography is something that should never be taken for granted.

3) *Consistency*

Thanks to the internet, and the ease of discoverability. Consistency is paramount.

An example of how to exercise the consistency in your personal branding is to arrange your username to be the same across all of the social media channels. This is a more memorable approach; it also makes it easier for people who are searching for you across the platforms. In order to surface the correct accounts quickly. Be sure that the username you choose reads professionally.

Think- MaxJMills across everything instead of Mr. Max8794, MaximilianxMills87, and MJM8794.

Besides your username, you should be employing a consistent headshot across all of your online accounts. This is also a best practice for personal branding. Since everything and everyone it now links on all the various and most popular social media platforms (particularly because we can use things like your Google profile on the social media platforms of a wide variety.) You can even import your Google profile. For instance, to shopping platforms such as Etsy and eBay and a wide variety of other platforms too numerous to mention here, it is highly important that your given market demographic be able to recognize your "brand" and/or profile on any platform where your present. Your brand may be everywhere, but if your chosen market demographics can't recognize you consistently, then you are doing nothing more than hurting your brand and slowing down the progress of its growth exponentially.

4) *Direction*

How will you recognize the smell of success when it comes? How do we recognize that you are making progress in building a quality well established recognizable personal brand when it happens?

Well, this is where the importance of direction comes in. Many of the most accomplished professionals, they have a clear sense of direction. This includes a long-term vision, with well-defined goals, and a solid foundation to drive your vision for your personal brand and its goals forward into the future.

Before you make any major personal brand maneuvers toward a specific goal plan, stop to think about the professional direction you want to then plan your next steps accordingly. It is vitally important to always come back to your goals and visions for your personal brand and make sure you are heading in the direction it is best to maintain the optimum vision for your personal brand, however. This can sometimes also mean being able to recognize the traditions or goals for your personal brand may change over time either for a personal change in your life or because your chosen market demographic is experiencing unique and unexpected changes. It is important to recognize when these changes occur and adjust for them. Accordingly, so as not to damage your hard-earned reputation and brand.

5) Evolutionary

Instagram, Old Spice, Pabst Blue Ribbon, - All of the companies that own these brands have hugely successful brand names. They have undergone remarkable rebranding over the years. Also, this says something about these companies' willingness to evolve and change over the years to keep their brands successful.

Much like these brands, it's important that you keep a close eye on the relevance and success of your approach of personal branding, and to change directions accordingly. Just because something works now for your brand for a little while, such as a profile on a specific social media platform or a specific brand image, does not mean that it will always work. Two years from now, or even as short as a month from now, it is important to recognize when a specific aspect of your brand is no longer reaching your chosen market demographics, as your brand should. Change your personal brand to a new platform image or advertising slogan. Do this to keep in touch with your given market demographic.

As you are developing new skills, you should think through how you would evolve your brand to consider that. Similarly, as certain mediums for promoting your brand fades out of favor, invest in new mediums. Your personal brand should be consistent, yet always evolving to reflect the most current, accurate representation of you.

6) *Focus*

Rome was not built in a day — and you shouldn't expect your personal brand to be. Establishing yourself as having expertise in your industry or a noteworthy resource for any subject requires a dedicated approach to delivering value to your audience while upholding your own values. Just like everything else in life, establishing a personal brand requires hard work, sweat, tears and long hours, and a willingness to adjust and go back to the drawing board. If something about your brand isn't working well, adjust it. Progress, slow and steady built it to reach a specific goal. Remind yourself of that fact every day. Exactly why you are trying to build a personal brand and set realistic goals. Small goals, so you can keep moving forward and making steady progress to establish a brand that will last for generations.

Don't expect results overnight. Focus on what you can do today instead, to strengthen your personal brand tomorrow. Remember, if establishing a brand was easy, then everyone would do it.

7) *Growth*

Consider the skills you already possess and the skills you want to build to advance your brand. If you have a fairly large skill gap to fill, to realize your desired outcome, it's important to have a plan for prioritization.

As you move towards conquering the skills on your "to-do" list, start by ranking each one by highest growth potential. Which skills do you need to tackle first to make the biggest impact on your overall brand? Which skills will help you grow the most? Start there.

8) *Human*

Think about the last time you scrolled through Twitter. We are willing to bet, that for every profound, original post from one of the folks you are following, there were about 20-30 automated tweets along with a blog post title and a link.

While there is nothing wrong with automating aspects of your online presence, your social, email outreach, etc. It is important that you're strategic about how you go about it. It is also important when you automate a process such as e-mail or social media is important to remember to keep up on the various changes that may occur within your given market demographic that might affect your personal brand and its reputation. Just because you automate a given aspect of your brand doesn't mean that a particular automation program will be effective to three months from now.

Here are a few rules of thumb to help you strike the right balance:

- **Don't: Share just a link to an article.** Instead, add color commentary. Share the article *and* share your thoughts on it.

- **Do: Ask questions of your audience.** No matter what your platform is, inviting your audience to participate in a conversation with you will help you get to know them. And better position yourself as a trusted authority.

- **Don't: Send the same pitch to everyone.** Take the time to do some research. The more personalized your outreach is, the more folks are willing to be giving you a shot. Whether it be a guest post, a consultation, etc...

9) *Interviews*

Here's a piece of sage advice: Say 'yes' to every single interview you're offered — whether it is aimed at a potential job, an article, a podcast, etc…

Depending on the interview, there are some prospective personal branding wins to gain by saying yes.

Job interviews ...

Even if you're not interested in the position offered, going through the interview process serves as a great purpose for practicing and refining your professional sales pitch of yourself. It provides you with an opportunity to sell yourself and your skills.

Also, the feedback you receive from the interviewer can be helpful in improving your personal brand. For example: if the interviewer questions the predominantly weak part of your resume, you can identify it as an opportunity for improvement or clarity of that part.

Podcasts or written interviews ...

If you are at ease with talking about your area of expertise or industry, obtaining an interview — whether it is written or auditory, is a perceptive way to gain exposure for your personal brand.

Depending on the spot you land, an interview can help you get your name in front of a large audience — one you may have not had access to otherwise. And many times, an interview can open doors for another opportunity. Momentum for the win.

10) _Join_

Thanks to the internet and social media, there is no shortage of professional groups to get involved with. And aside from the obvious networking aspect, joining these groups can be particularly helpful when it comes to expanding the reach of your personal brand.

How so?

Joining a community or group centered on something you're passionate about and want to be known for can help you:

- _Develop new skills_
- _Improve ideas_
- _Establish yourself as a resource_
- _Gain inspiration..._

If you're not exactly sure where to start, visit your favorite social media platform or for and type in the best keywords you can think of; you want to associate with your personal brand and/or if given market demographic. This will help you find a group and/or community that will allow you to add to your cooperative network. Skillset, knowledge, and outreach for your personal brand.

11) *Knowledge*

It is important to remember that, your personal brand is rooted in your knowledge or passion in any area. This knowledge can go a long way in benefitting you to establish credibility with an audience. It is vital to becoming a part of the community in your chosen market demographic. This means spending time on forums, e-mails, listening to blogs and reading articles, and spending time with your community and establishing a respected presence within that community. It is crucial to building a successful personal brand. No one will respect you if you don't walk the walk if you talked the talk.

If you have a personal website, we recommend it for anyone looking to advance their personal brand, to use that as a platform for highlighting your expertise. Also to use it to share information with others. By volunteering your insight through blog posts, eBooks, or case studies, you are showing your willingness to help.

12) _Leadership_

Anyone in leadership positions will tell you, personal branding comes with the territory of being a leader. Think about it: It's important that you commit to developing yourself first. You do that before you prove that you can help others develop in their own careers, right?

This means knowing your strengths and weaknesses, honing your emotional intelligence, understanding how you like to receive feedback, and so on. These aspects contribute to your style of leadership. Which ultimately plays a role in defining your personal brand.

13) _Mission_

It's the best practice for companies to define a mission statement. The mission statement sets the stage for what the company does. And, perhaps more importantly, why they do it. The mission statement serves as a guiding light. It pushes those in the organization to uphold the company's values, purpose, and principles.

When it comes to your personal branding, defining a mission statement, one which is specific to your professional development can be equally effective also. Before you sit down to write yours, take some time to reflect on the following questions:

- *What are your personal career goals?*
- *What core values do you hold?*
- *What does success look like to you?*
- *What are you most passionate about? and Why?*

14) *Network*

Want to earn guest posting slots, speaking gigs, and/or even awards and recognition? These personal branding milestones - require that you start by doing one thing: meeting people.

By networking and building relationships regularly, you are consistently inviting new people in. These new people have the potential to shape your brand by offering you new opportunities for personal and professional growth.

Need help kick-starting your networking schedule? HubSpot's Chief People Officer Katie Burke suggests playing "Eventbrite Roulette." She suggests to "Search for events happening in your area in the upcoming week and attend the third-event that shows up on the page," Playing this type of event roulette is another way to build your skill sets, knowledge, and personal network. It gets you into interacting with your chosen community and market demographic that your personal brand is on target towards.

15) *Opinion*

Many people withdrawal from infusing their opinion into their personal brand, as they worry that they might alienate or offend part of their audience. Or they will say something that would be construed as being offensive. This is a valid concern, however, sticking to sweeping generalizations and careful word choice can and does hold your personal brand back.

Part of establishing a personal brand influence means that you owe yourself a chance to take a stance on the issues that matter the most to you. Depending on your line of work, there is certainly room for your opinion. and having it as a defining aspect of your personal brand. It is important to remember the reason a personal brand works and is effective, with the given market demographics and audience. It is the fact that they value your opinion on a particular subject or area of expertise. Otherwise, why would they care about your brand in the first place?

The key to success here is to, share your opinion. But, share your opinion alongside with your experience. This technique of communication helps others understand where you are coming from. Also, it opens the doors for conversation around the subjects. However, it is important to be open to new ideas and embrace the experiences and thoughts of your audience as well. As you share your opinions, this will help you establish better long-term credibility with your given market demographic.

16) *Public Speaking*

Regardless of whether you're comfortable with speaking or not, public speaking is a tried-and-true way in which you can broaden your personal brand. Speaking engagements help to position you as an authority or expert in your market area or industry. These engagements help to expand your network of contacts and earn the trust of a new audience also.

Feeling a little shaky? Here are a few tips. Some of which ensures that your next speaking gig serves as a positive reflection of your personal brand:

Speak about something you know inside and out. The more comfortable you are with the subject; the more conversational things will feel. Speaking about something familiar lends itself well to personal experiences and stories of which helps to humanize you as being a real person.

Know your audience. While you should always focus on being your real self, recognizing who your audience is, helps you better direct your content. As an example, your humor may land you with one group, but not another. Know when you need to pull back certain personality traits.

Get feedback. Practice your talk in front of a group of coworkers, you trust before taking the stage. Running through your talk in advance helps you feel more confident in your delivery. It also brings to light any areas you need to work on your speech.

17) Quirkiness

One way to impart your personal brand with some individuality is to use your quirks — the little things that set you apart from others. For example, maybe you are known for calculating complicated math problems in your head, doodling in your notes, or not being as graceful as would like to be.

Whatever your quirks may be, don't be afraid to incorporate them into your personal brand. While they may seem senseless - they do make it easier for people to relate to you. Your quirks provide a level of interest and intrigue about you. Let your personal geek flag fly. Be willing to embrace your fellow geeks as well, as they salute your flags with open arms. Quirkiness and uniqueness are what will help your personal brand stand out from the millions of other individuals. That are in your market demographic will come across on your favorite search engine or social media platform. Remember you want to establish brand loyalty in a market demographics, and the best way to do that is to show your personality, warts and all to your audience.

18) *Reputation*

With a reputation as part of your personal branding efforts - There are two key areas you want to focus on:

1. Your online reputation

The process for making many major decisions starts with a Google search. And as with your personal brand also. Your online presence will reveal a lot about you, your work, and what it's like to work with you.

To keep tabs on your online reputation, set up a Google Alert for your name. This is so you receive a notification every time you appear in a piece of content. This is a great way to track positive mentions of your name and your brand. This is also while keeping a close eye on problems you may need to resolve.

2. Your offline reputation

Several factors determine your offline reputation. This includes - The quality of your work. The way you treat others. The way you react and respond to feedback, and the influence you have made on other people. Like we mentioned earlier - It takes time to build up a quality reputation, and only seconds to lose it. So, whether you are online or off - It is important that you put your best image forward and freely embrace it. The opinions and feelings of the individuals that make up your market and demographics, try not to take any negative criticism personally. It is better to embrace negative criticism and feedback as a learning experience. This is so you can help to make your personal brand the best it can be, rather than to view negative feedback as a personal attack.

To achieve a positive outcome in these areas, you need to be committed to constant improvement. To achieve this, you do it by tapping into your self-awareness and self-regulation. This is to ensure you are putting your best foot forward.

19) *Social Media*

For many, personal brands and social media on the internet go hand in hand. So, if you want to establish your personal brand, you need to establish a social media presence in which to support it.

That being said, simply having social profiles, that you post to regularly, is not enough. You have to be strategic about your social output. What you post, when you post, and why you post that? Ensure that it reflects the behaviors and values that are anchored in your personal brand.

Here are a few of our favorite tips for using social media, in which to advance your brand:

- **Follow the people you admire.** Ask yourself - what types of content are they posting? How often are they posting? And how do they engage with their audience and followers? Make note of what their strategy is and look for ways that you can incorporate them into your own.

- **Align - your title, username, and headshot across the multiple social media platforms.** We mentioned this up in the consistency section, but it bears repeating. Make it easy for folks to identify you and what you do. Do this by maintaining consistent identifiers across your multiple accounts.

- **Post often.** Part of building a memorable brand boils down to properly setting expectations. Commit to posting at least once a day on particular channels so people can rely on you for consistent, fresh updates.

20) *Trust*

A great way to build trust and advance your personal brand. This is to ask to write a recommendation or testimonial from those you have a strong professional relationship with. So that, you can then use these writings across your website or social accounts. Others who got it like this the behavior has become, for better or worse, a giant popularity contest.

The algorithms on most (if not all) of the most used social media platforms are based on the popularity of a brand or its content. Meaning that the more people who have positively reviewed your website, video blog, post, or article; the easier it will be for someone in your given market demographic to find you. This is by performing in organic search (typing in specific keywords) to find your brand. So, the more positive feedback you gain, the more visible your personal brand will become. However, again, building positive feedback is one of those things that you have to stay on top of. Losing a positive rating can do more damage to your brand and your business faster than just about anything else.

Stumped on whom to ask for a testimonial? Try to get a variety of people - managers, folks you manage, contacts at other companies you've worked closely with, etc.

21) *Unique Value Proposition*

As a professional, *what problem do you solve? What value do you add? How do you make a difference?*

Asking yourself questions like these above will help you determine your value proposition. Which is a fundamental piece of your strategy for your personal branding.

Think of your unique value proposition as the key differentiator that people will use to evaluate your personal brand and determine what makes you the most qualified person to do XYZ. You can use this on your resume, in a LinkedIn summary, or on your professional website.

22) *Visibility*

Once you have a foundation for your personal brand, it's time to spread the word.

Onc of the best ways to increase your visibility is through a calculated content strategy, where you are focusing on delivering your special value through the social mediums that are important to your audience. This could be through courses, blog posts, video content, email campaigns, webinars, etc...

Whatever form of visibility you choose, it is important to remember to be honest with your audience be yourself and let your personal brand shine through as it is your unique perspective and values that attract your audience to your brand.

23) *Well-rounded*

This category may seem a little confusing at first., your personal brand is centered around the *one thing* you do well. Better than everyone else, correct?

In most cases, the answer is yes. You want to become known for what you do best — for example being a seasoned pastry chef or an expert in classical music, or whatever it is you do best, etc... However, while there are advantages to knowing and owning your niche. There are advantages to also maintaining a basic understanding of a variety of unrelated topics.

Why waste brainpower on broadening your knowledge? It's simple: Knowing a bit about everything makes you more relatable. It makes it easy for you to talk to people, which makes it easier for you to build connections that will advance your personal brand.

24) *X-Factor*

Similar to your unique value proposition, your "*x-factor*" is the thing you bring to the market that your competitors or other folks in your industry do not have. Think of it as your very own disruptor.

Maybe you have access to a vast network of influencers that are willing to work with you on projects. Or you may have been recognized as the top content marketer of the year for many years running. Whatever your "x-factor" is, it is your job to incorporate it into your personal brand.

25) *Year*

We will admit it, coming up with a term for 'Y' was more than a little challenging, but this is a term that is actually important.

Make a conscious effort to update all of your personal branding assets -- resume, professional bio, LinkedIn summary, author bio, personal website, etc. -- on a yearly basis as a best practice for maintaining an up-to-date professional narrative.

If nothing else, this will help you avoid all of those "Oh sorry, I don't work there anymore" emails.

26) *Zealous*

If you've made it this far, well, we are impressed. Thank you for sticking with us.

You must act like you are in pursuit of the Holy Grail when it comes to building your personal branding knowledge. You must be prepared to eat and sleep personal branding information. To devote countless hours and even possibly lose a little sleep to gaining personal brand knowledge so that your personal brand can be a shining star and a beacon of intrigue in an ocean of individuals trying to establish a quality, long-lasting, personal brand.